Adult Coloring book South West & Floral

Vol 2

By: L. M. Boelz

pages

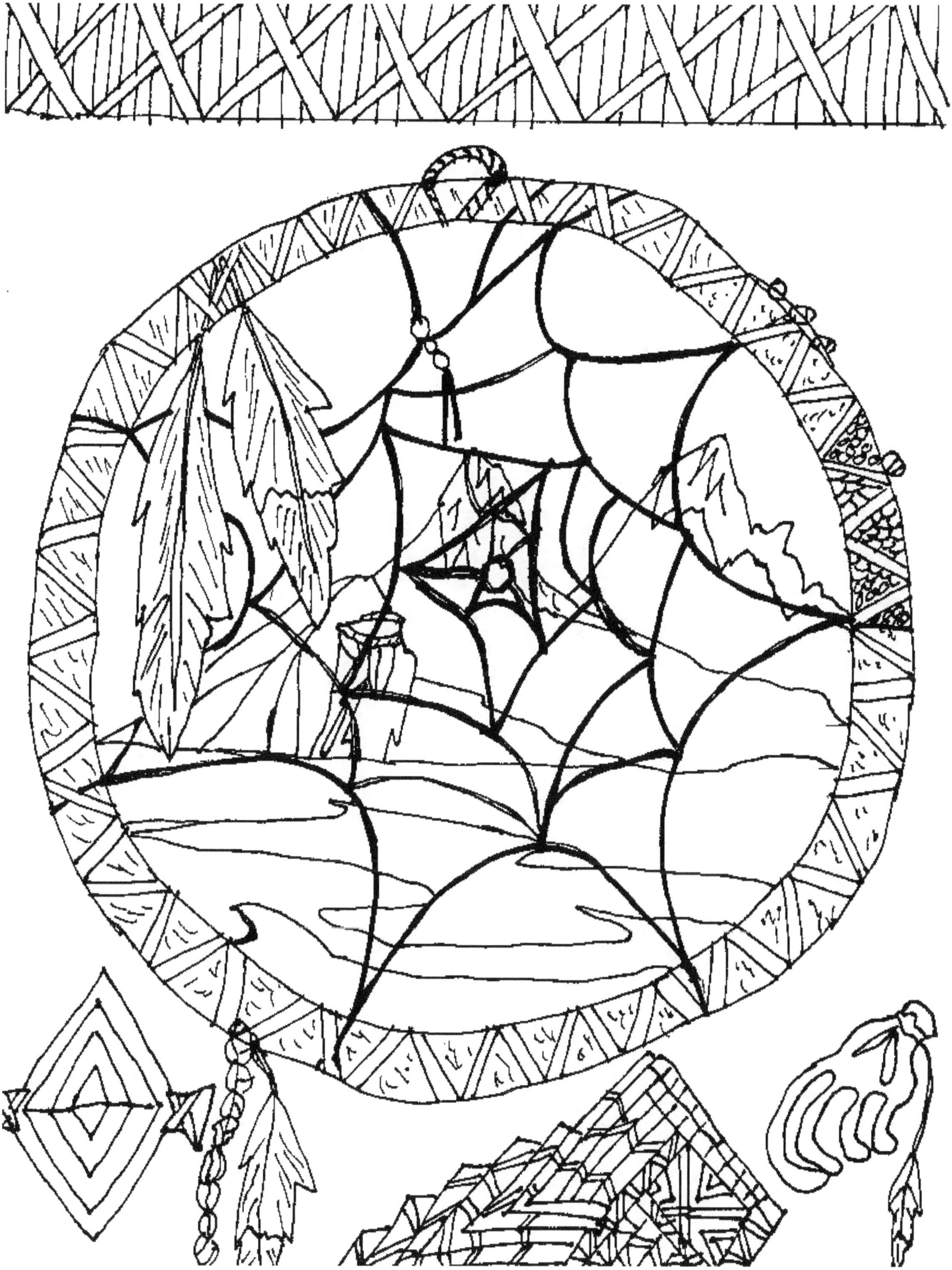

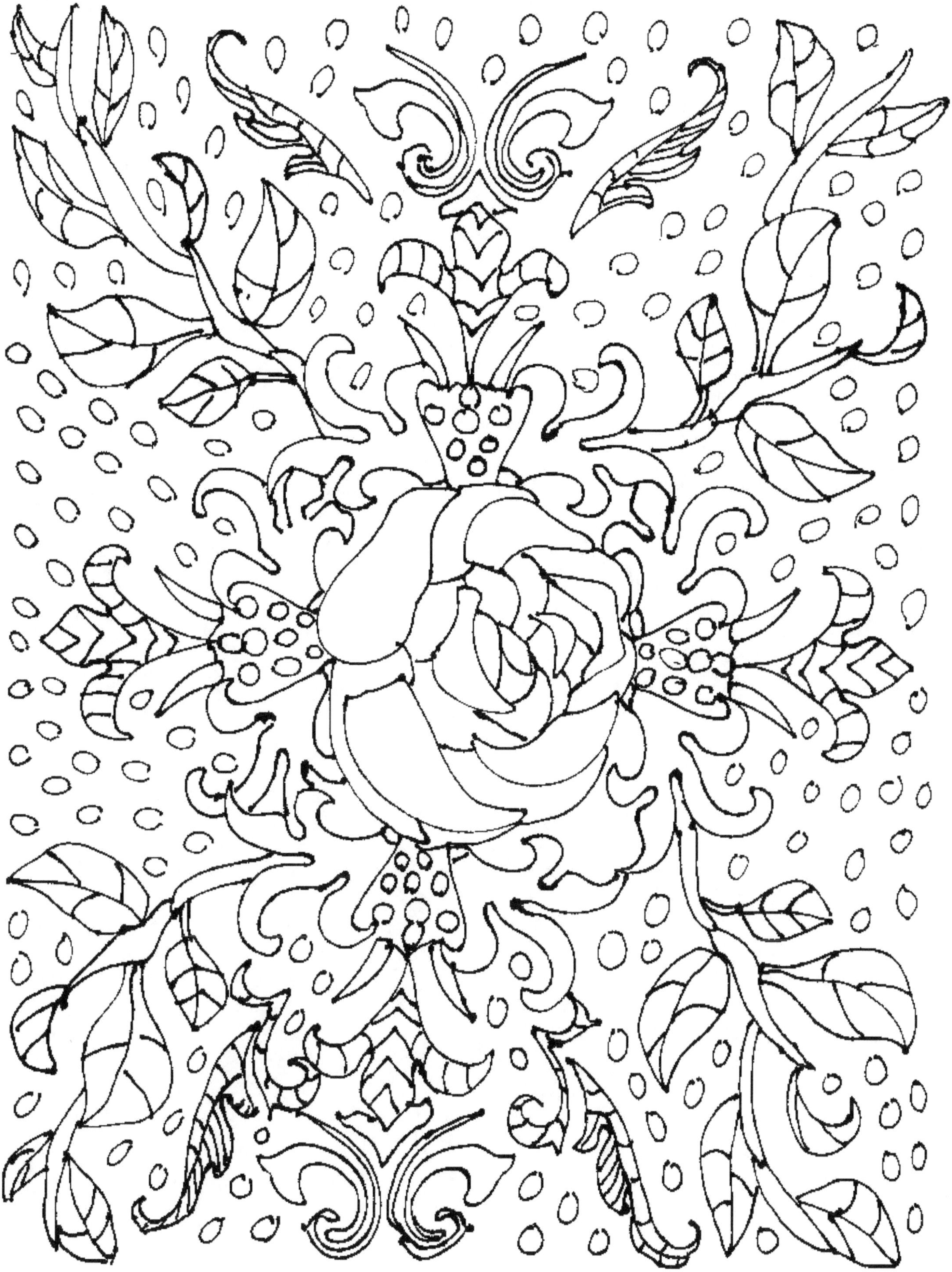

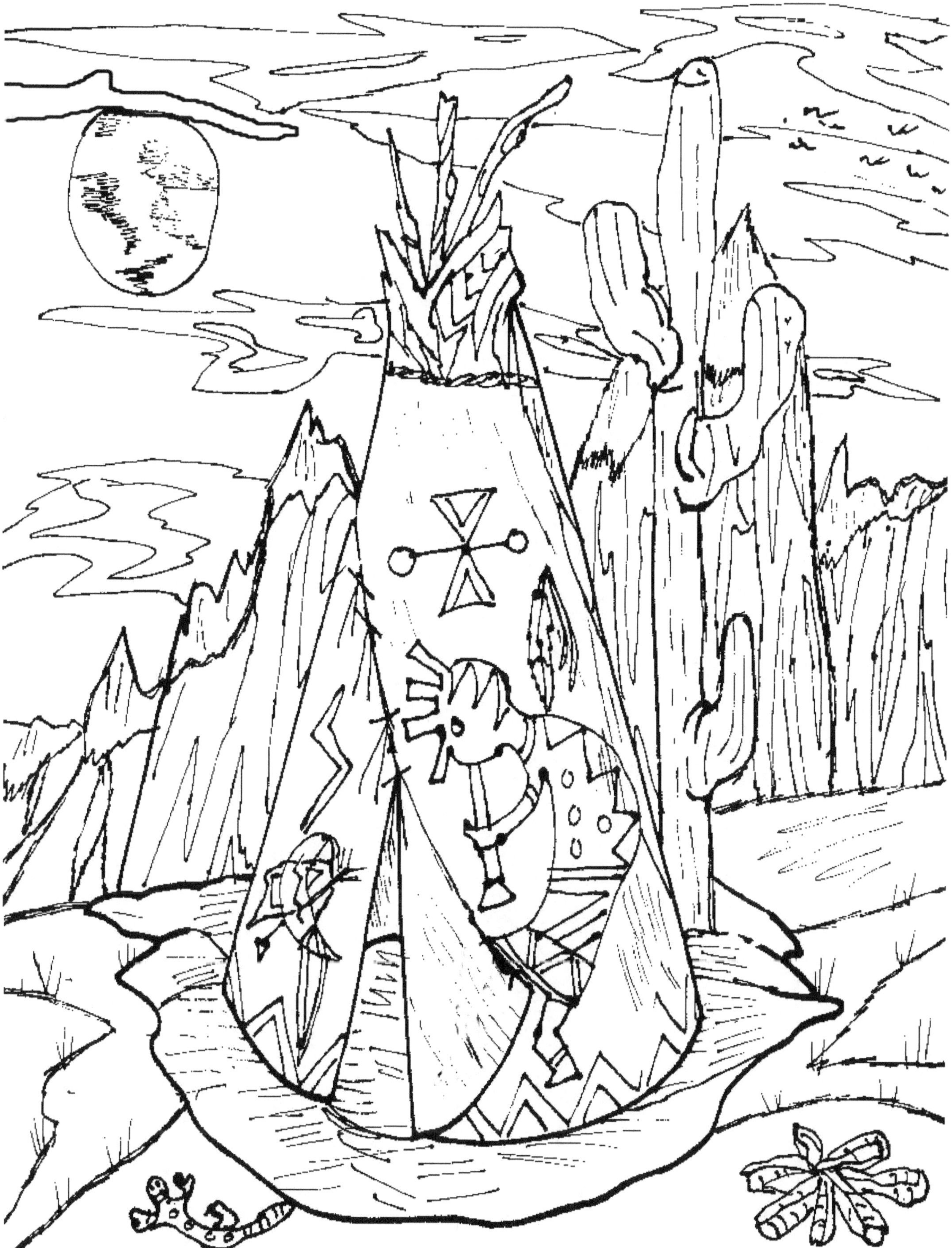

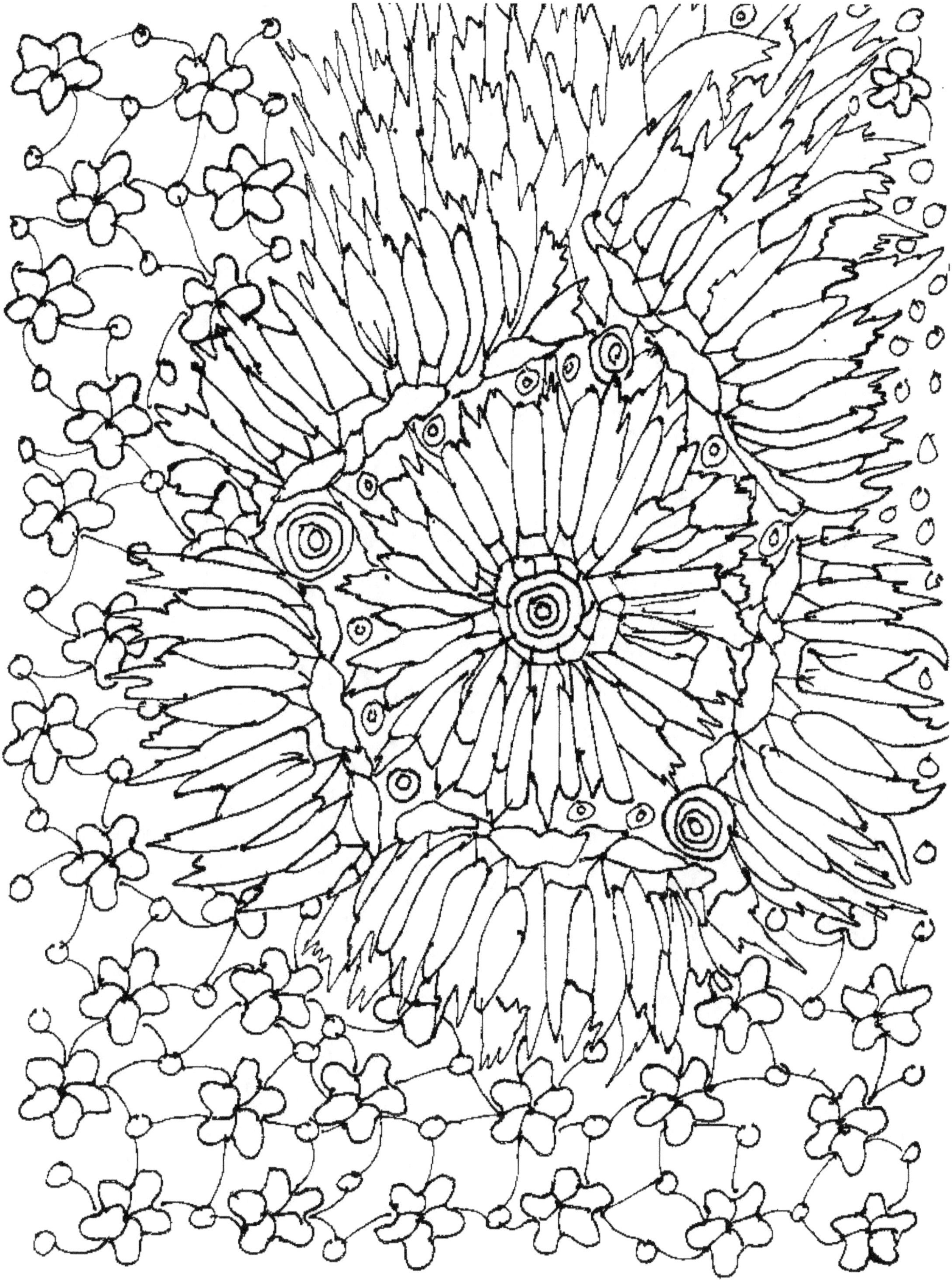

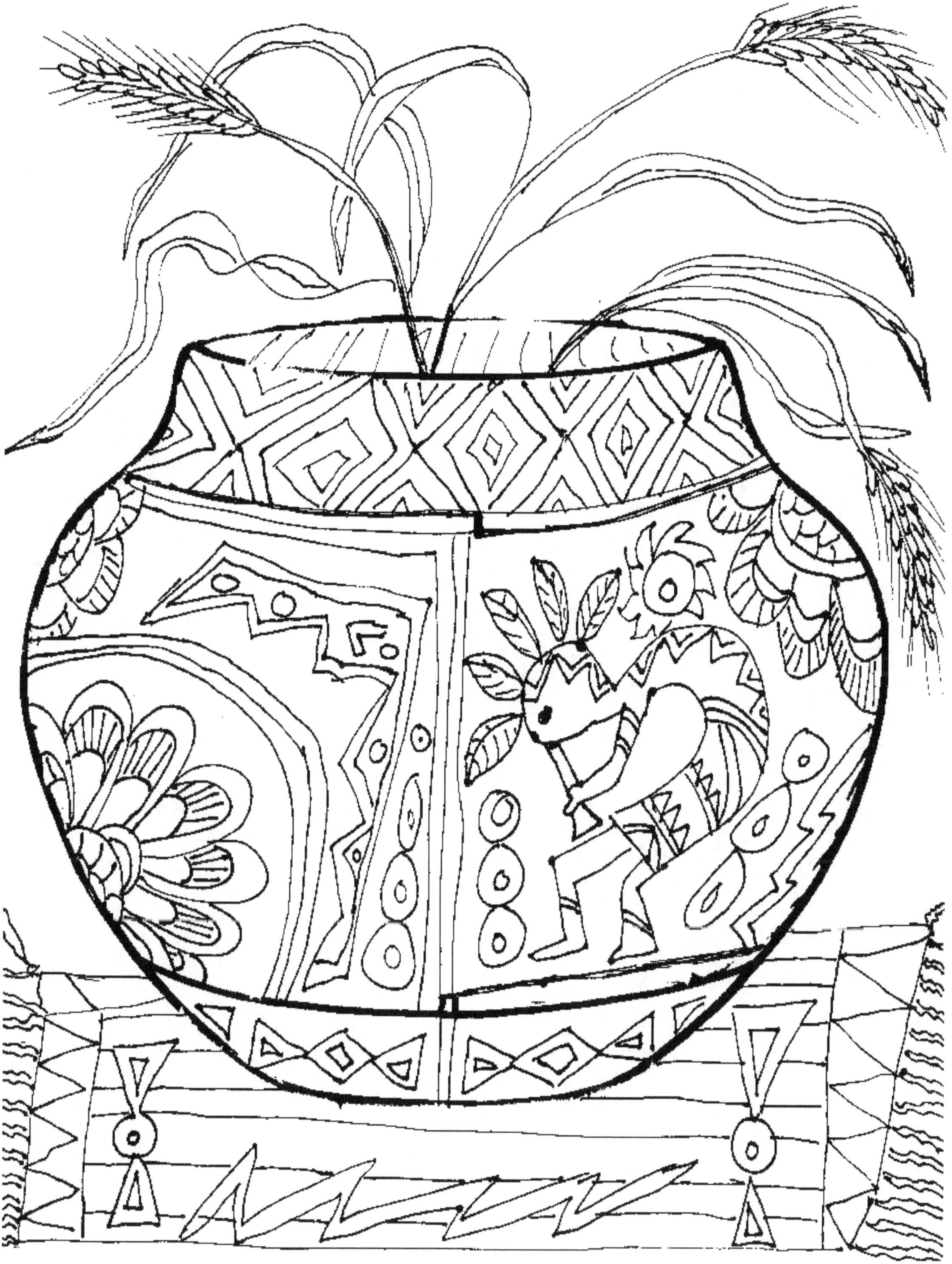

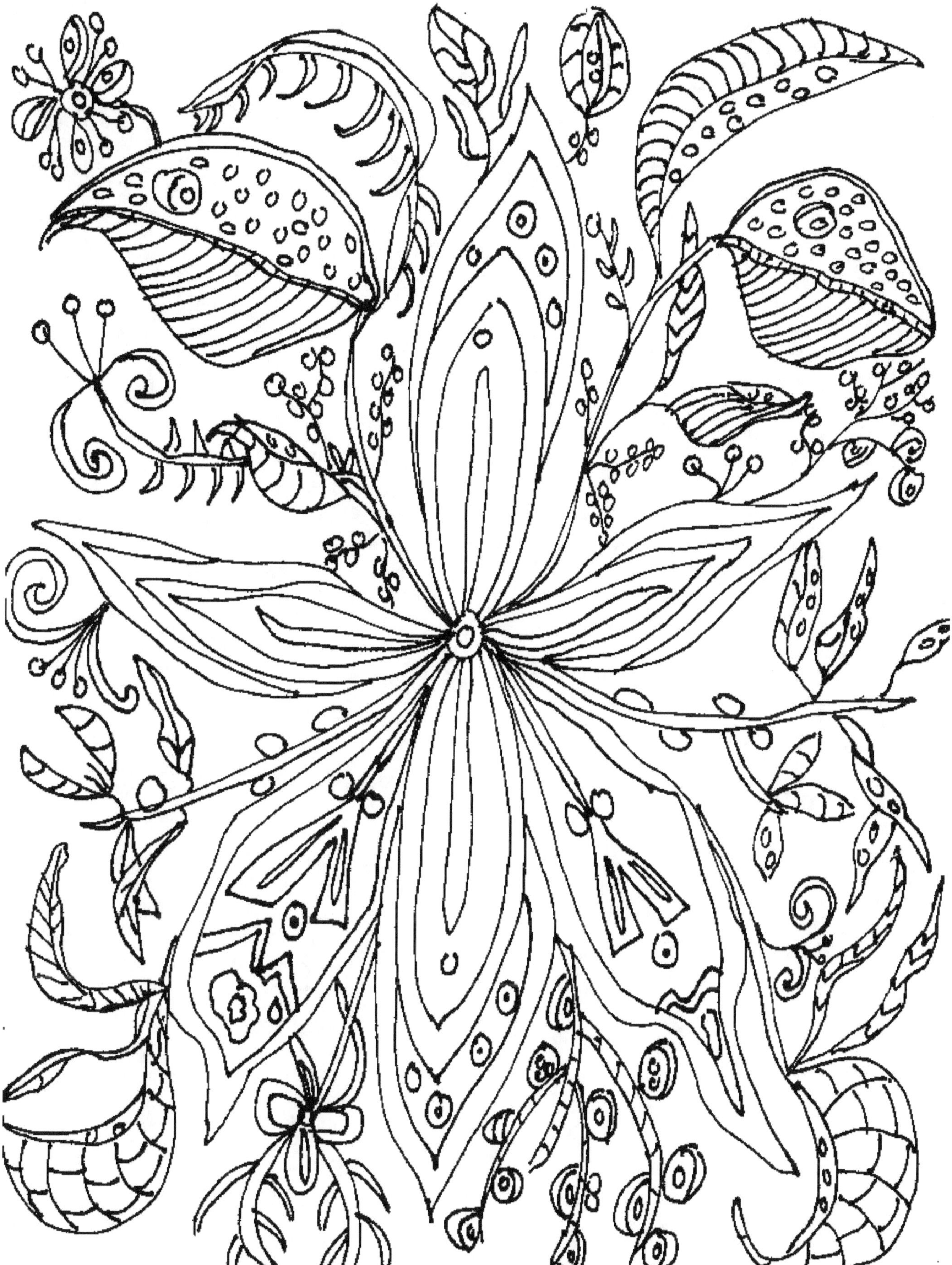

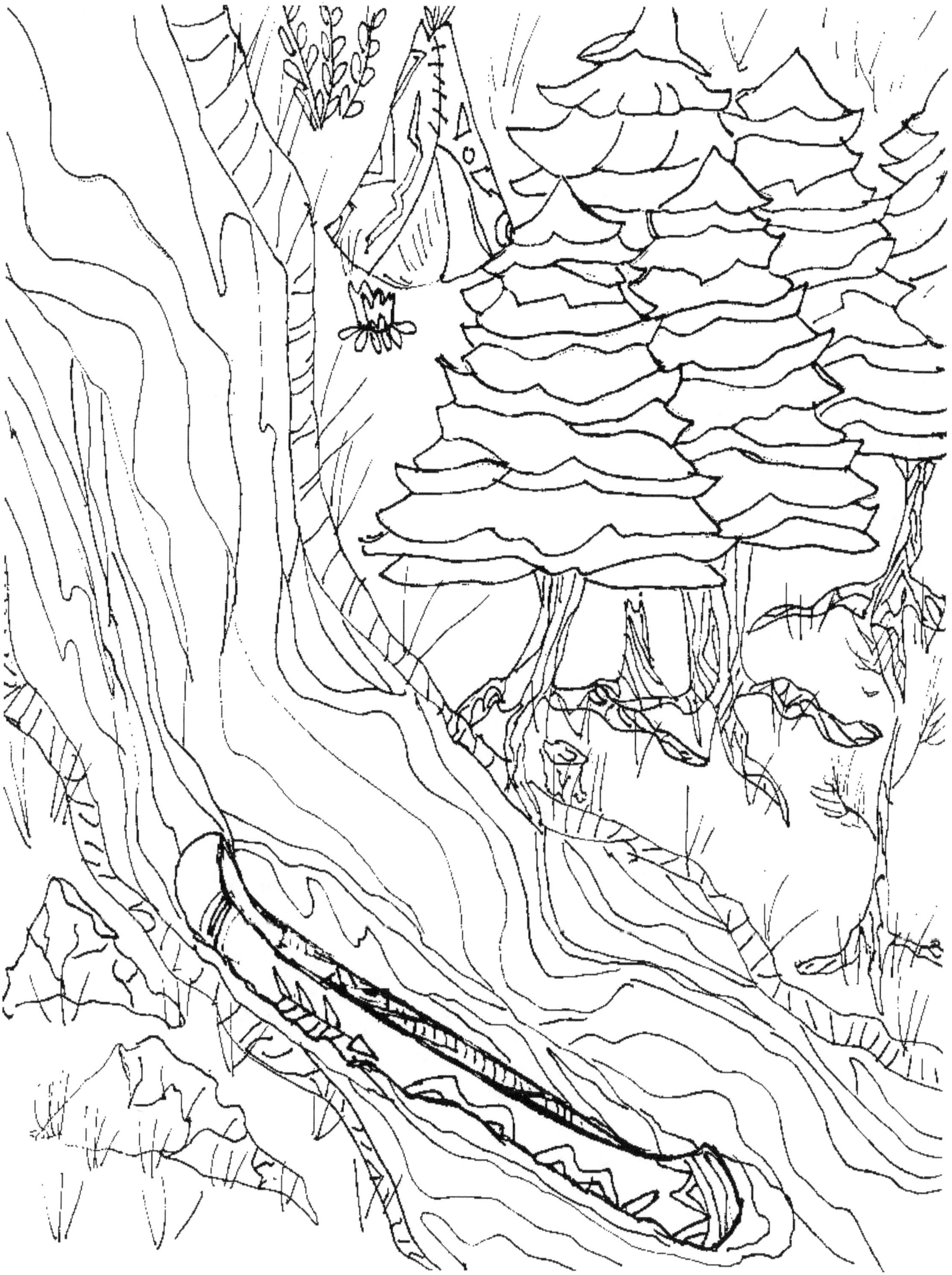

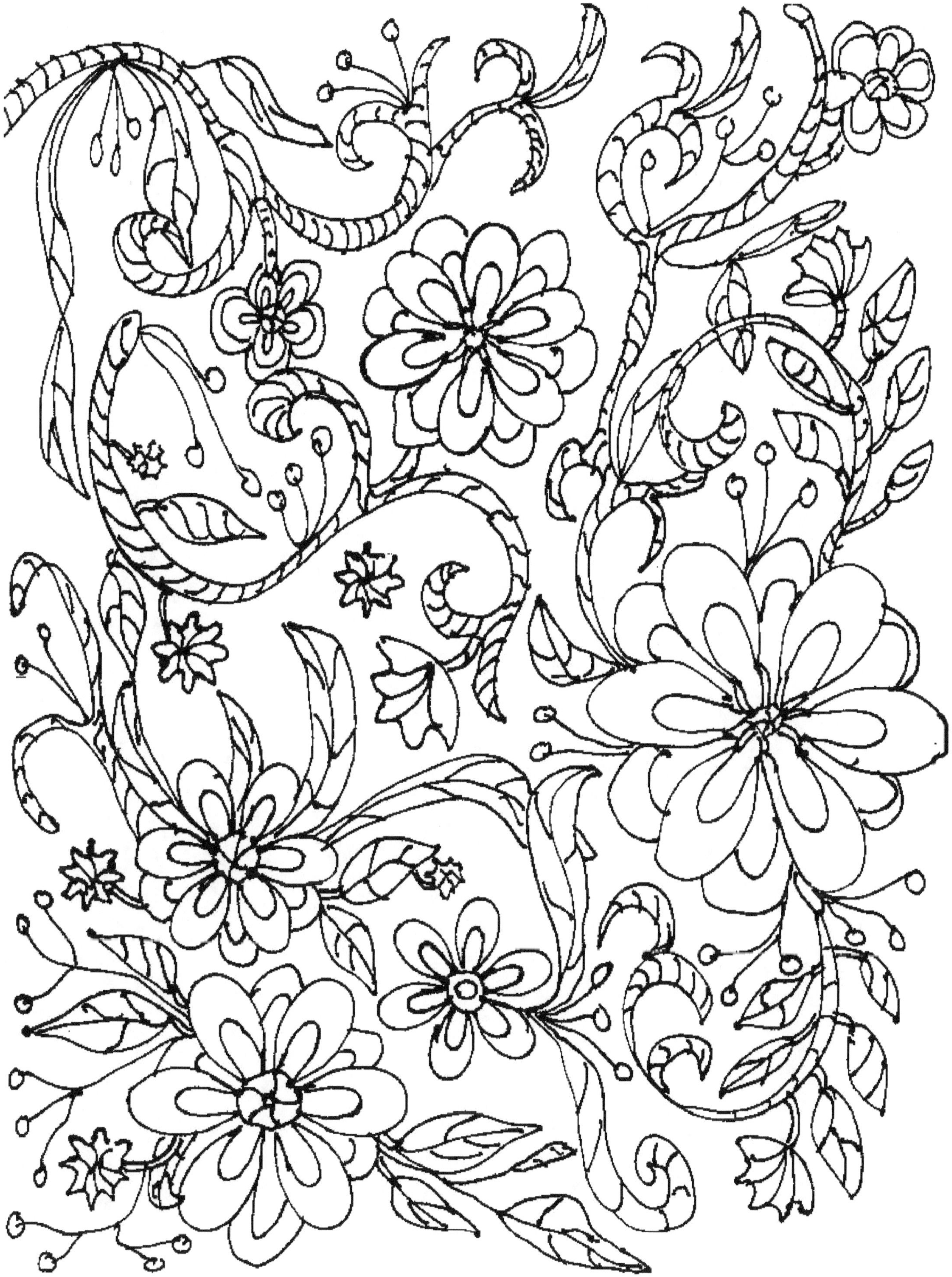

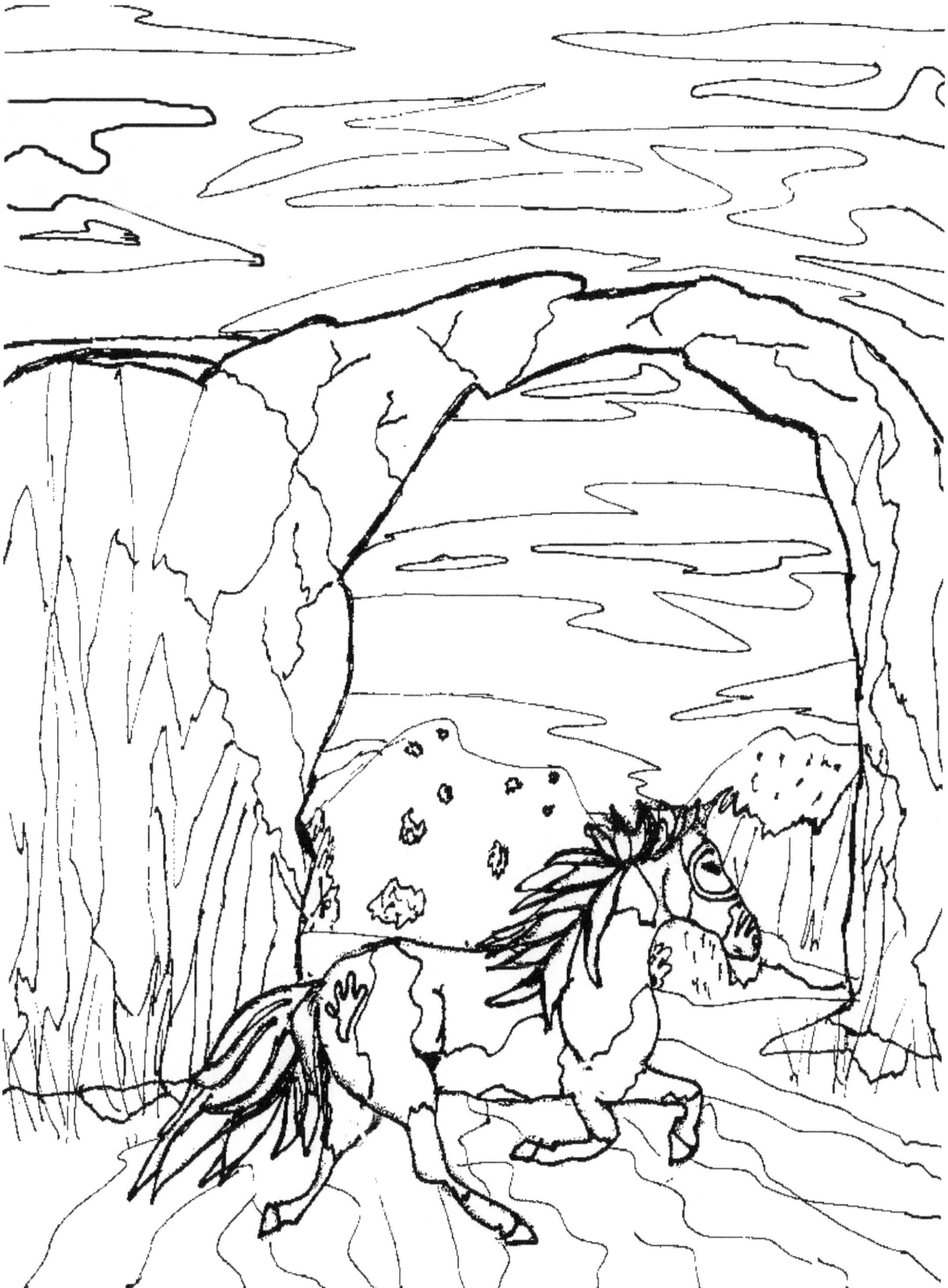

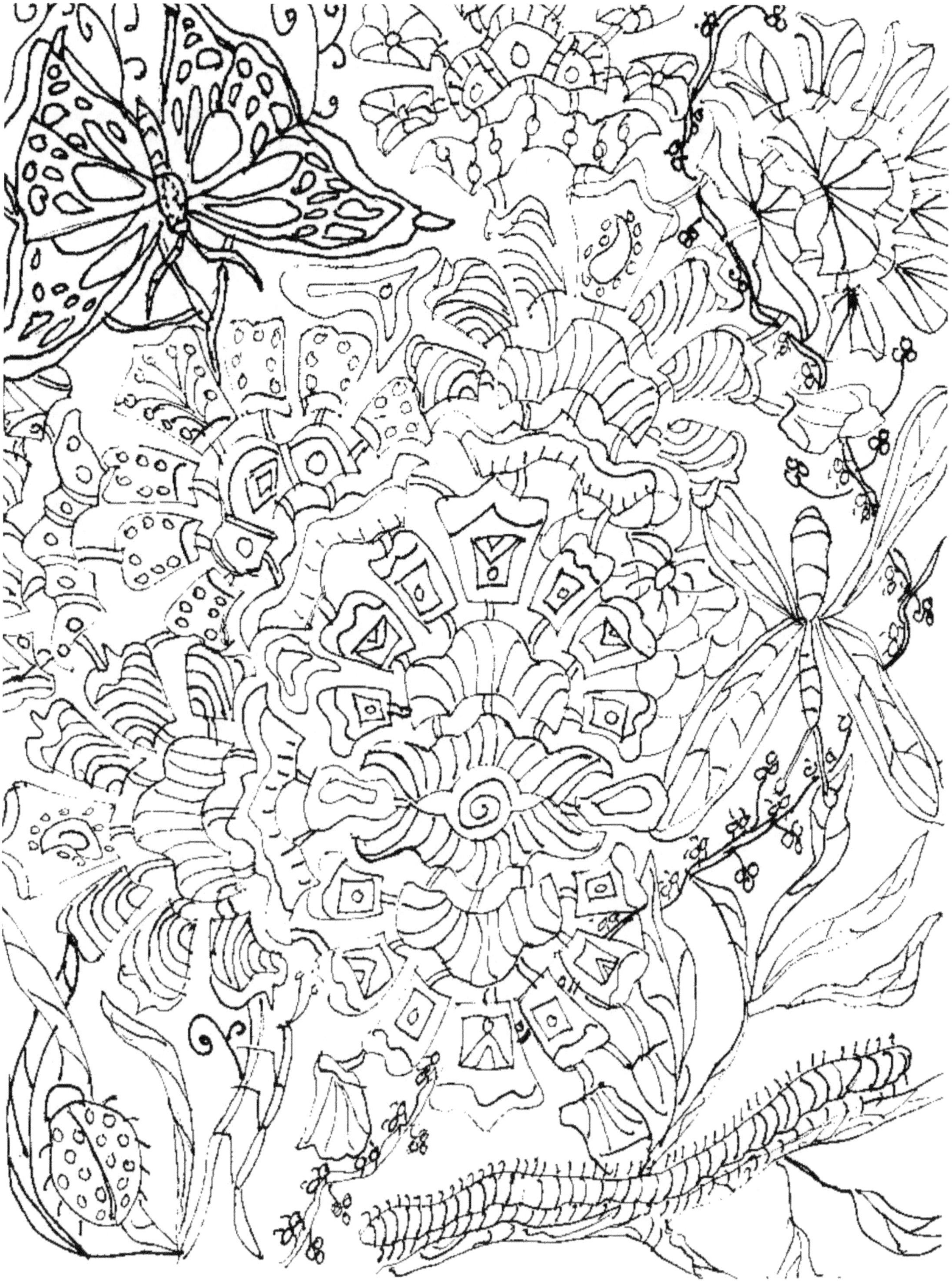

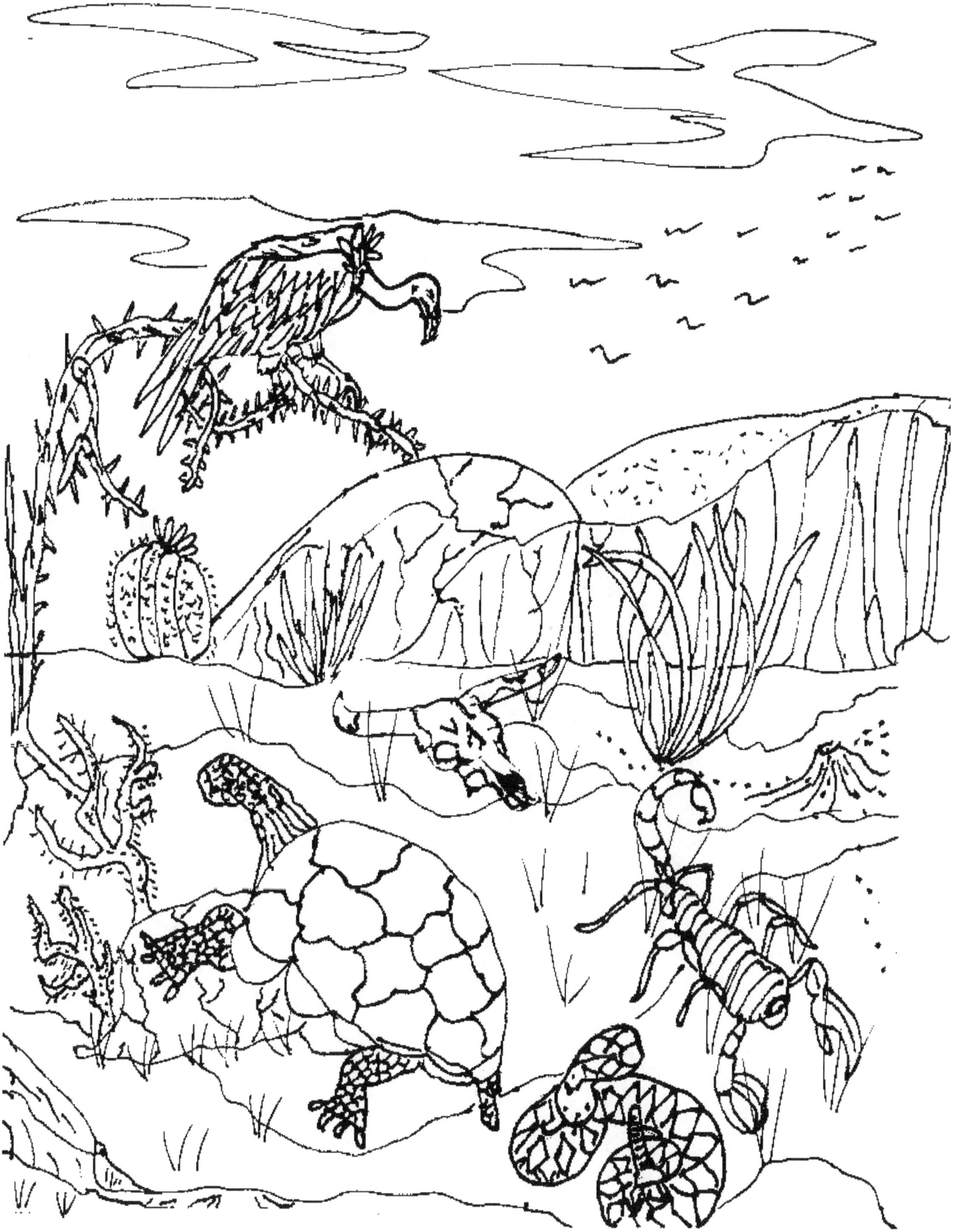

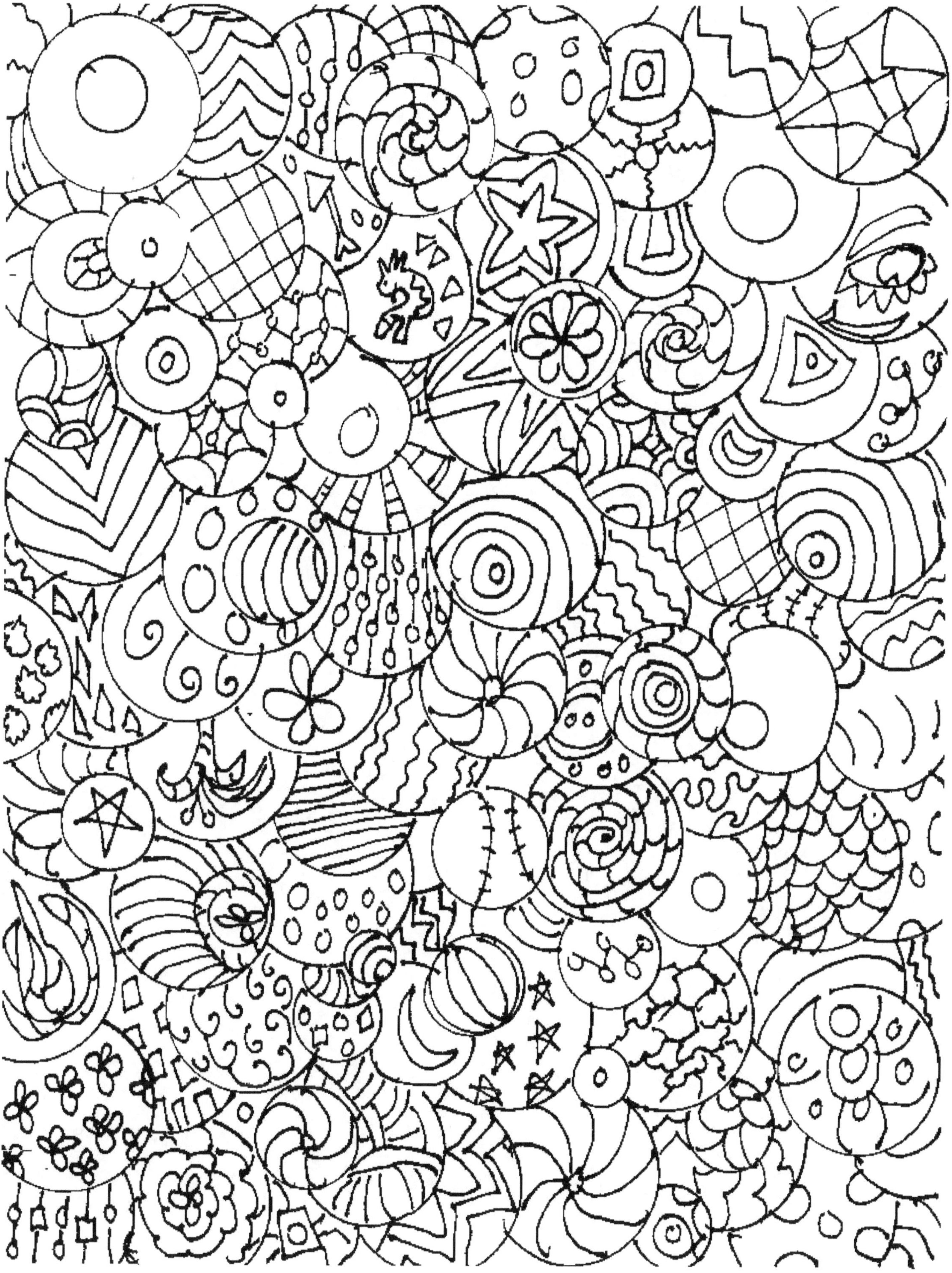

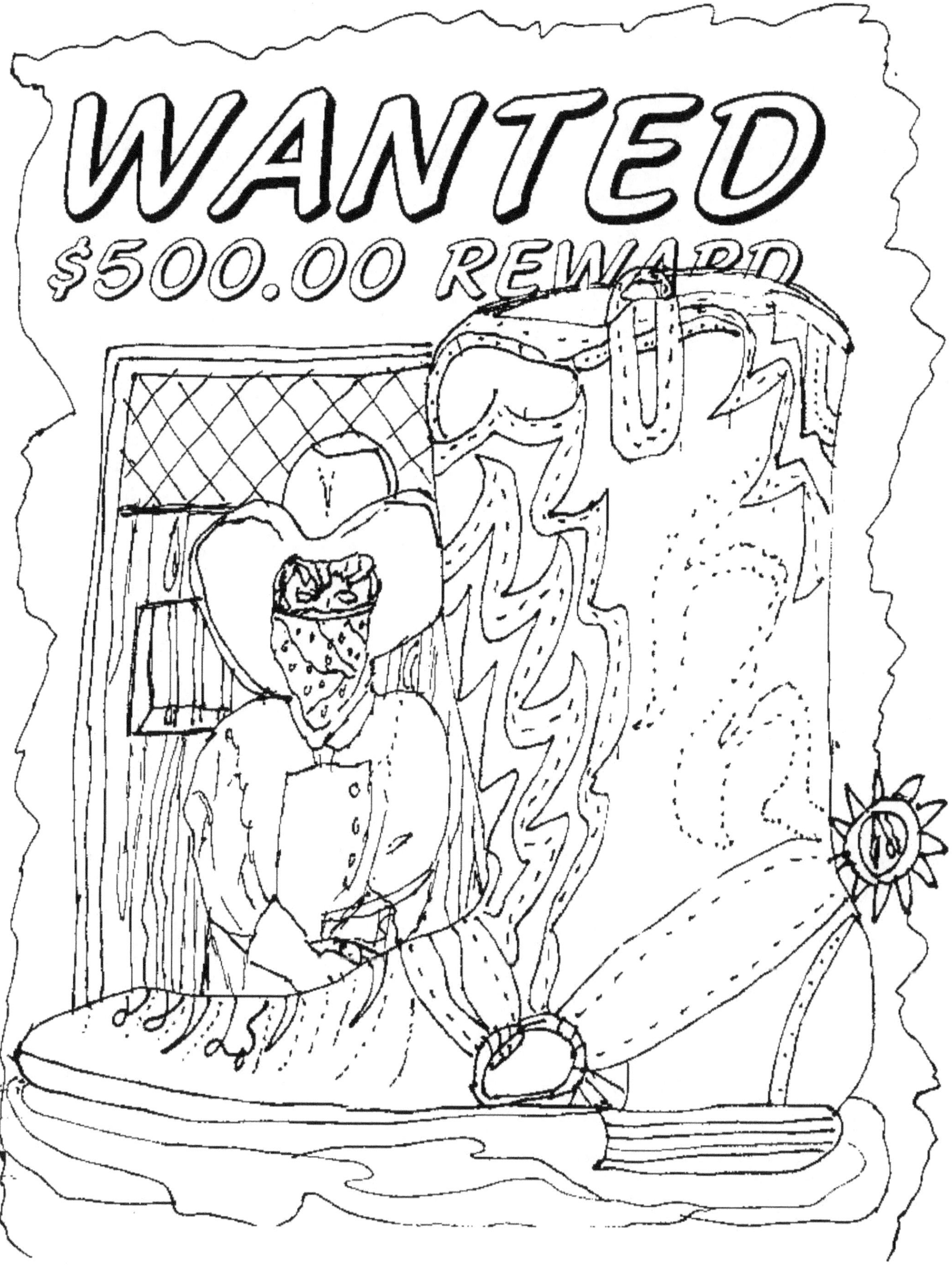
WANTED
$500.00 REWARD

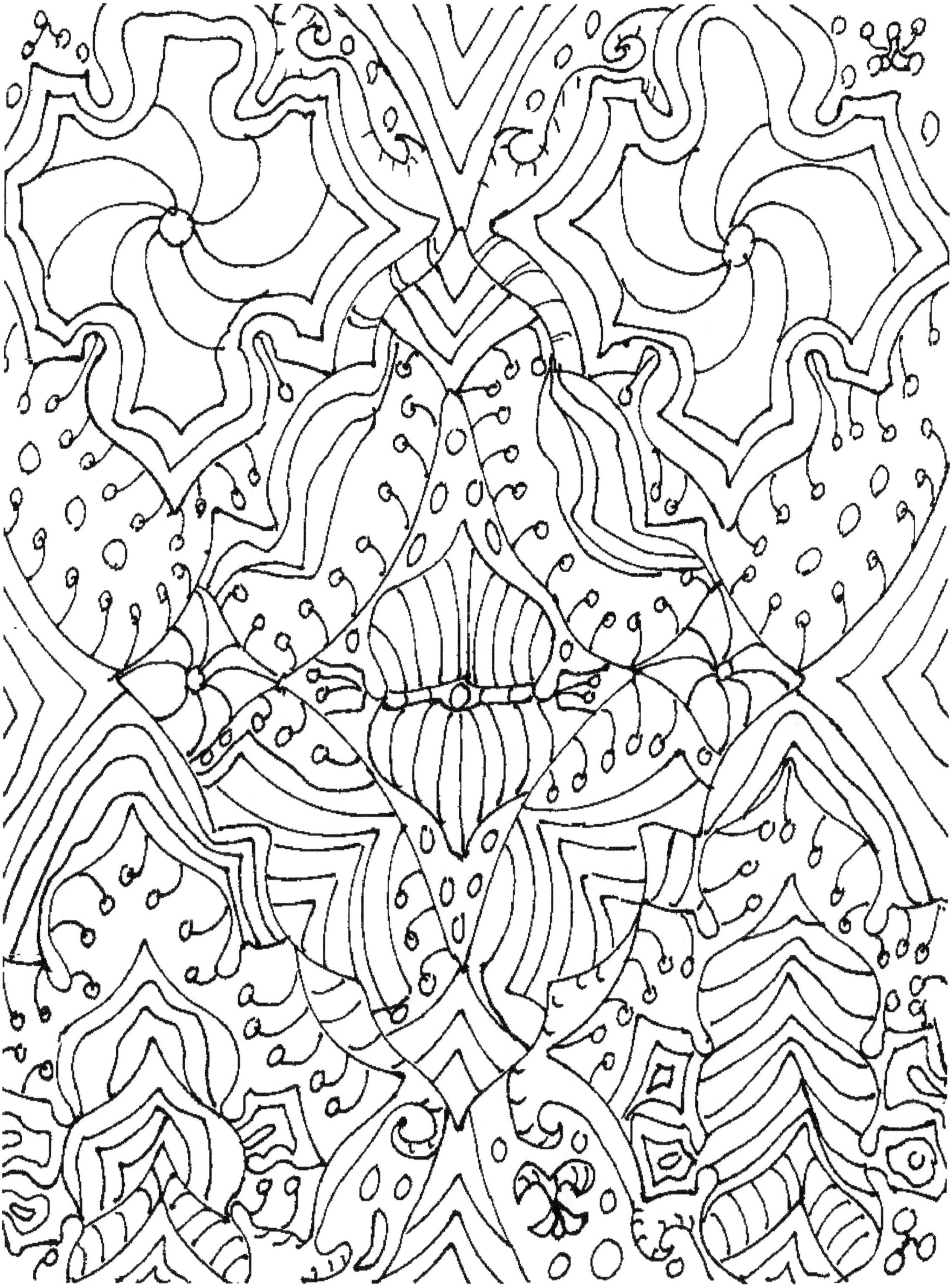

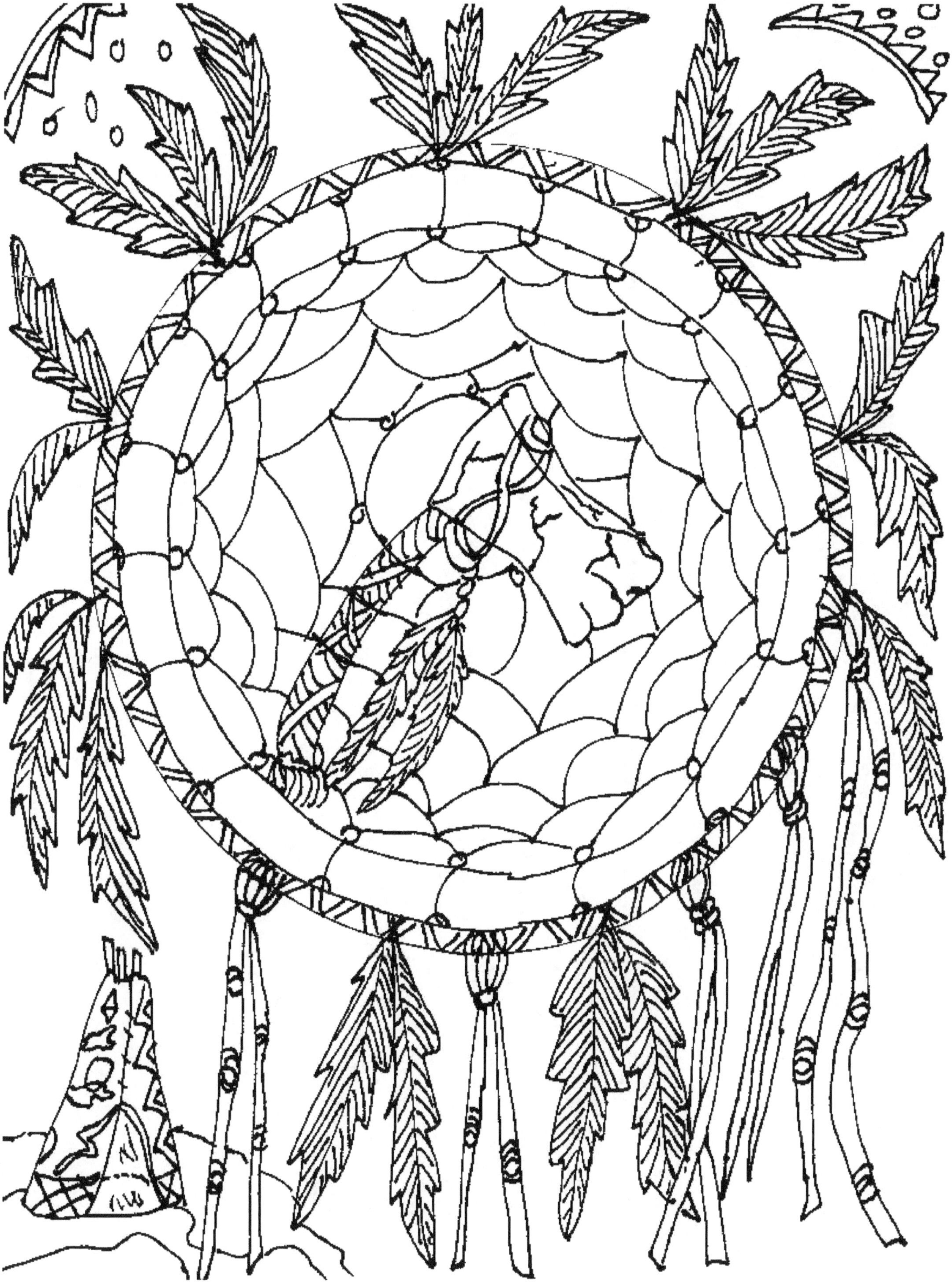

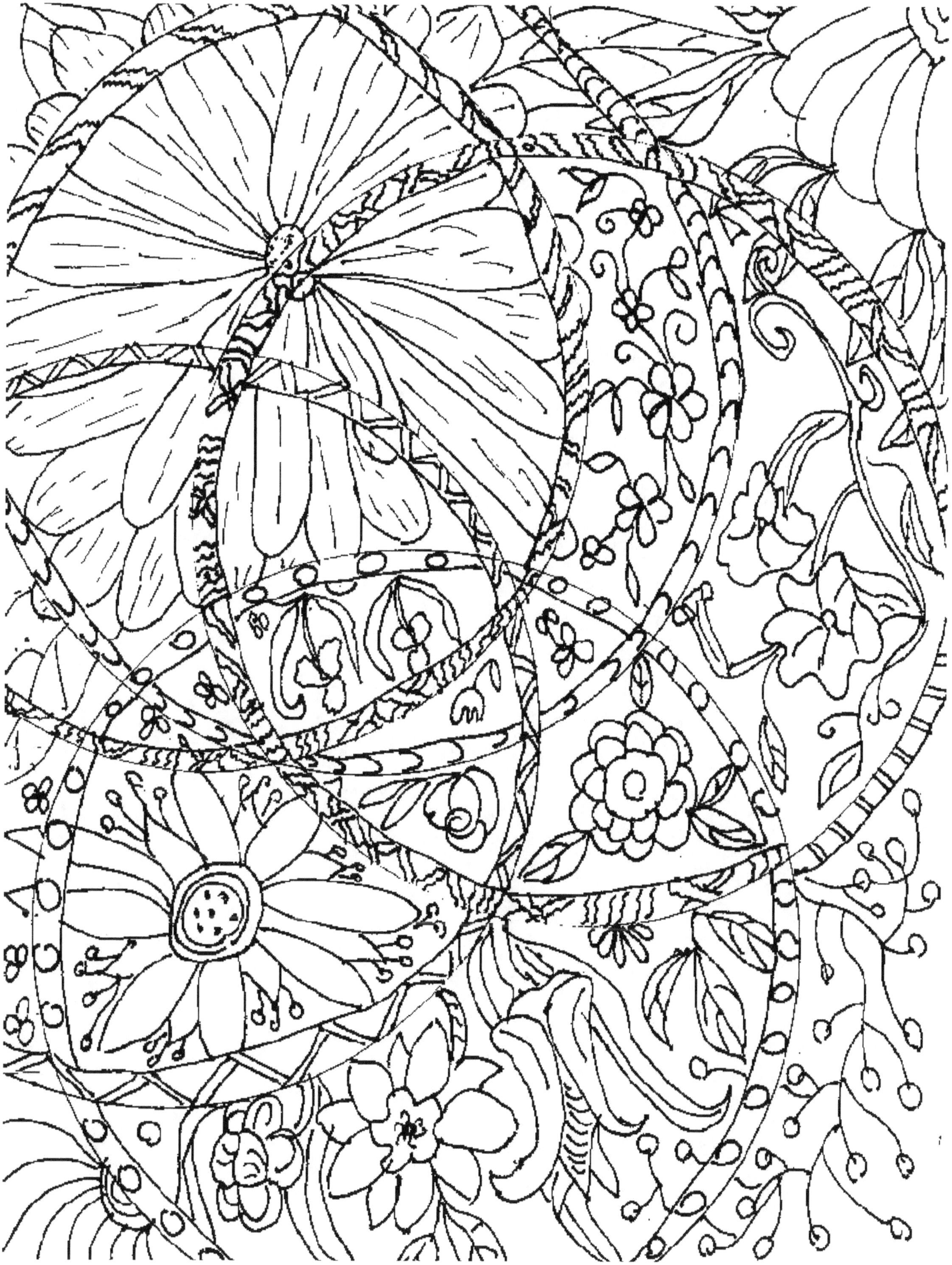

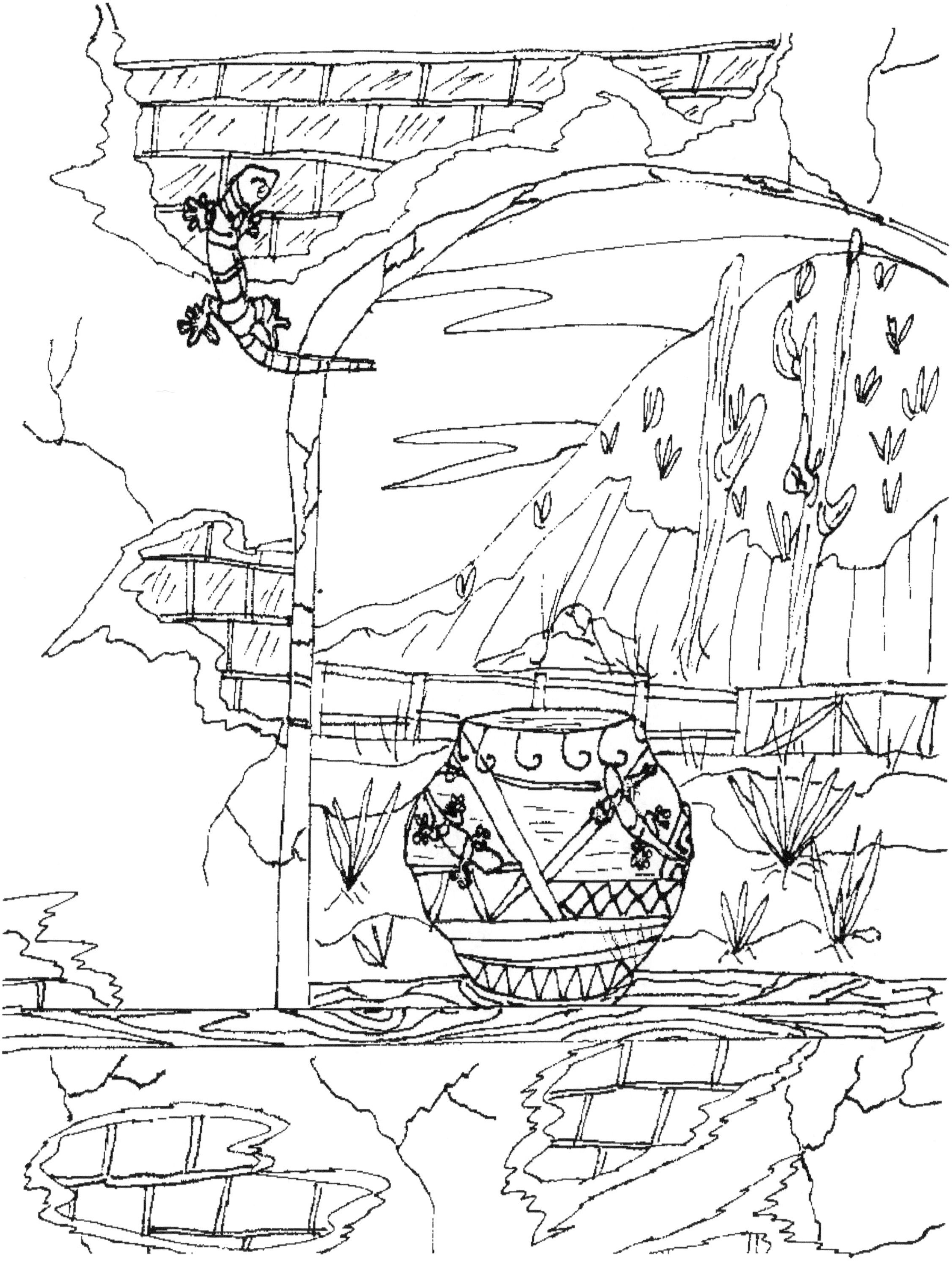

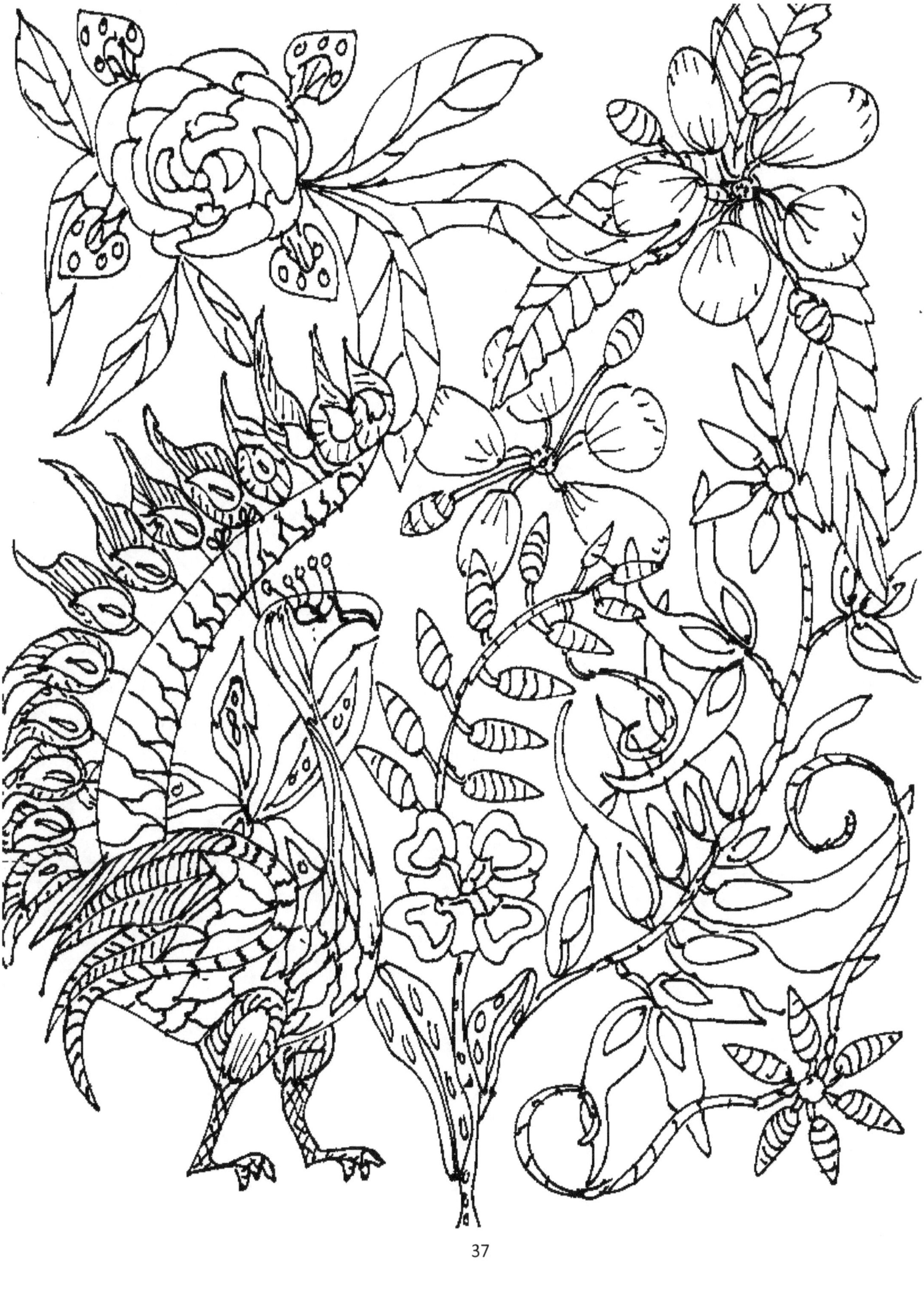

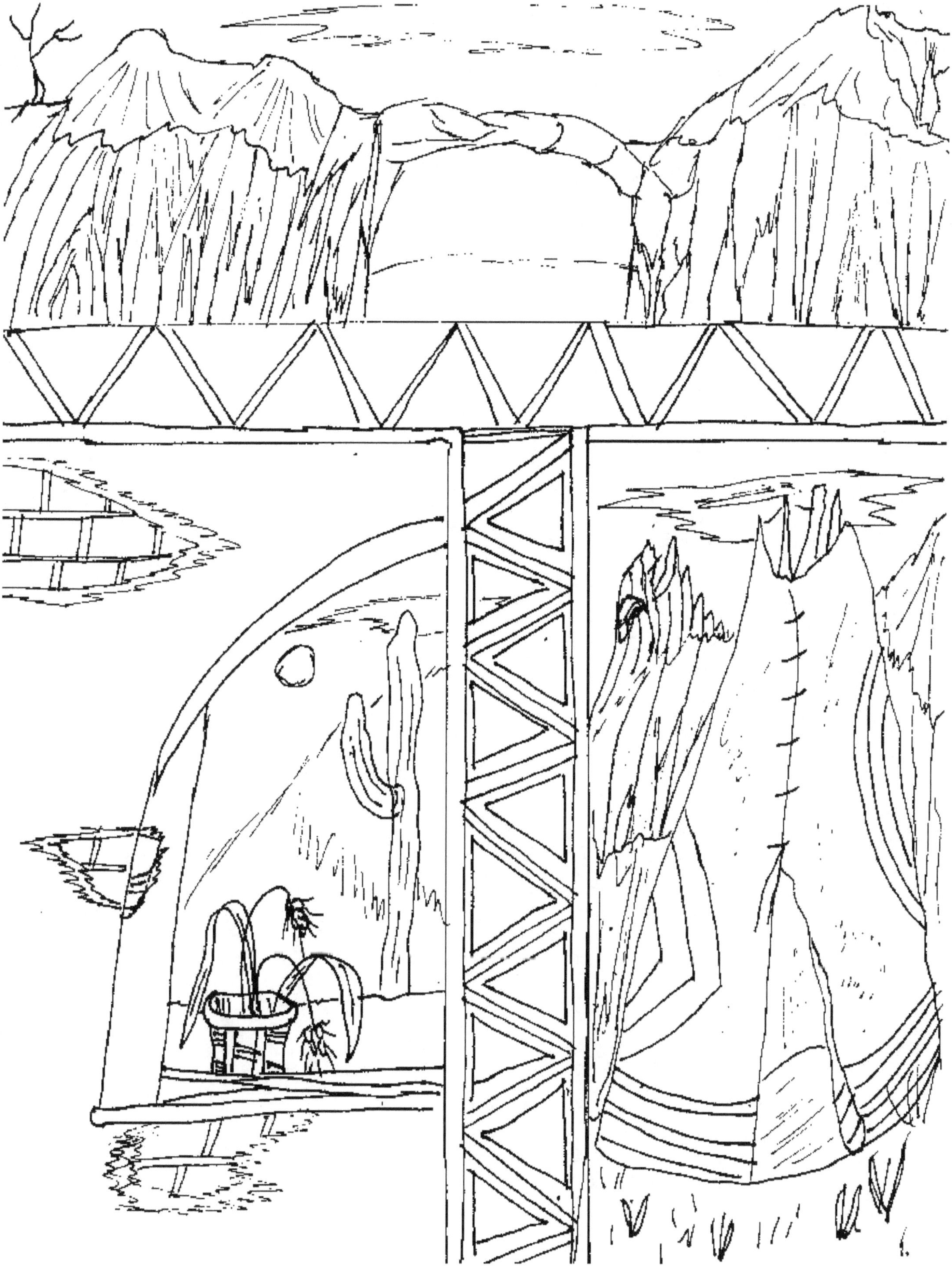

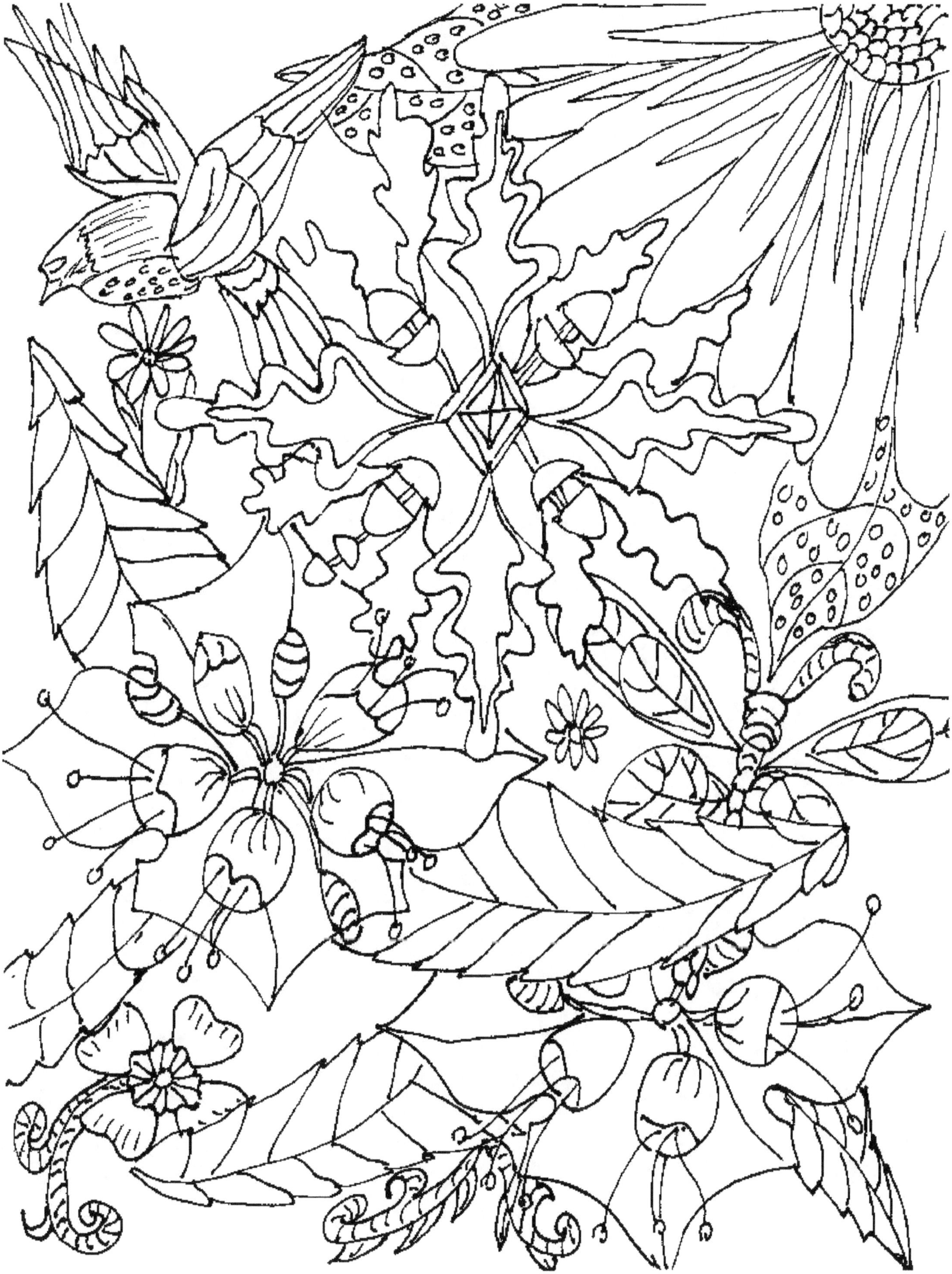

www.ingramcontent.com/pod-product-compliance
Lightning Source LLC
Chambersburg PA
CBHW080615190526
45169CB00007B/3019
* 9 7 8 1 5 2 3 8 6 7 9 6 7 *